52 Weeks of Purposeful Thinking

Robin A. Hill

52 Weeks of Purposeful Thinking
Copyright © 2022 Robin A. Hill

All rights reserved. No part of this publication may be reproduced, distributed, or transmitted in any form or by any means, including photocopying, recording, or other electronic or mechanical methods, without the prior written permission of the publisher, except in the case of brief quotations embodied in critical reviews and certain other noncommercial uses permitted by copyright law. Permission requests should be sent to info@writewaypublishing.com.

Printed in the United States of America
ISBN 978-1-956543-21-6 (Paperback)
ISBN 978-1-956543-24-7(Hardcover)

Book design by CSinclaire Write-Design LLC
Cover design by Myke D. Etheredge

This book is dedicated
to my grandchildren
Isaiah, Maya, Nyomi, and **Natasha Robin.**

God bless all of you
with many years of purposeful thinking
and a quality, happy, successful life.

CONTENTS

INTRODUCTION — vii

JANUARY — 1

FEBRUARY — 13

MARCH — 23

APRIL — 33

MAY — 43

JUNE — 53

JULY — 65

AUGUST — 75

SEPTEMBER — 87

OCTOBER — 97

NOVEMBER — 107

DECEMBER — 119

ABOUT THE AUTHOR — 125

INTRODUCTION

THERE ARE MANY distracting circumstances that steer us away from focusing on the things that are most needful in our life. If you ask someone what their most needful things are, people from different walks of life and different life experiences more than likely will have different answers. However, people on their deathbed worldwide will probably have the same answer: "Take care of yourself, show the people in your life that you love them, and make the wrong that you have done right."

The goal of *52 Weeks of Purposeful Thinking* is to help keep YOU a priority in your life. Like the person who is valuing their last breath, take on every day as if it is your last day. Practice being productive in caring for yourself, loving others, and keeping things copacetic. *52 Weeks of Purposeful Thinking* encourages taking the opportunity to adopt right thinking. It encourages creating wonderful new habits. It is a step-by-step guide to accomplishing your goals, dreams, and desires.

I have taken some snippets from my book, *Urban Joy Ever After*, and my second book, *The Making of a Beast*. They represent my core beliefs that I want to share with you, so unless otherwise noted the quotes and daily thought topics are mine. My prayer is that you will find *52 Weeks of Purposeful Thinking* to be a helpful resource in accomplishing your goals and fulfilling your dreams.

Before diving in, make sure you keep a favorite pen and a special journal handy. Part of our process together will include you creating lists, laying out plans, and jotting notes about your thoughts, feelings, and actions. Somehow, the act of writing your thoughts down really seems to reinforce their importance and effectiveness!

Are you ready to experience a fantastic journey of redirecting your future to live your best life every day? If your answer is yes, let's get started.

52 Weeks of Purposeful Thinking

JANUARY

Week One

Look forward to the windows of your dreams being wiped clean as the sunshine of joy lightens the path of fulfilling them.

Week Two

Making excuses is a waste of life, time, and energy.

Week Three

Wasted time will never be reimbursed and will never propel you forward.

Week Four

*Joy is always positive—
always positive is life being joyful.*

Week Five

Stay positive and detach from negativity.

JANUARY: Week One

Look forward to the windows of your dreams being wiped clean as the sunshine of joy lightens the path to fulfilling them.
— Robin A. Hill

IT'S THE FIRST day of January, and you have mixed feelings. You are divided, feeling happy and feeling a little sad. You are happy that you made it to another year, but sad for those who did not. You feel really good about your accomplishments of the past year, but you feel behind schedule for the goals you did not reach. You feel one year older and a little wiser. Though 365 days have expired, you still have not conquered what you know in your heart you can. Trials, tribulations, challenges, and obstacles have muddied the windows of your dreams.

It's time to wipe those windows clean. Take a few minutes every day this week to practice being joyful. Joy is so powerful. *Without your permission, joy opens the door and invites hope to come in.* Mentally, let bygones be bygones. Yesterday is history. Last year is gone—unless you bring it to life in your imagination. Let your imagination be filled with dreaming about fulfilling your destiny. Your joy will lighten the path of your journey.

DAY 1
Today say goodbye to the obstacles and dissatisfactions of your past. No more thinking about them. Focus on your new day and new year only. In your journal on separate pages, list three to five goals or changes you want to focus on this year. Come back to these pages from time to time and note how you are progressing.

DAY 2
Today tell yourself to look forward to a new, accomplished, healthy, prosperous year. In your journal, make a list of things you are especially looking forward to this year.

DAY 3
Today dream about who and what you will become this year. Write down your ideas in your journal.

DAY 4
Today in your journal list at least one specific action you intend to accomplish to improve your life in these five areas: mentally, physically, socially, emotionally, and financially this coming year. This list can grow and change over the years. Revisit this list periodically and write your accomplishments.

DAY 5
Today choose a time to stop everything for 30 minutes. No smartphone, TV, or talking. Meditate on your progress during Days 1-4. Take time to understand your intentions. Dream about your possibilities. Make notes in your journal.

DAY 6
Today have a blessed and no-stress day.

DAY 7
Today just rest.

JANUARY: Week Two

Making excuses is a waste of life, time, and energy.

WOW! YOU HAVE made it through week one. Give yourself a hand. If you did not follow every instruction in week one, do not make one excuse. Let this year be a year of no excuses. It is useless making excuses. This is a year that you are going to commit yourself to do what you mean to do and mean what you say. It's not too late to accomplish anything you missed in week one.

When you open your eyes every day, you are starting with a clean canvas. Create your portrait to be whoever you want to be, void of excuses. Innately, we all have gifts, talents, and infinite creative abilities. This week give some thought to who you are. You may even discover more things about yourself. If you are getting excited, good! You should be. You have a lot to look forward to.

DAY 1
When you commit to doing something, do you usually fulfill that commitment? Write in your journal why you are or why you are not successful in fulfilling commitments you make.

DAY 2
Today review the list of what you intend to accomplish from last week. Make a list of steps for how you intend to accomplish at least two of the goals most important to you.

DAY 3
Today take the first step of your plan in one area from the list you reviewed yesterday. Do not let anything stop you. Your old habits will try and bully you. Do not listen. You are strong.

DAY 4

Today do something specific on your improvement plan list toward fulfilling your plan. Does taking an action step yesterday and today motivate you to keep moving forward long term on completing these plans? Write about this in your journal.

DAY 5

Today choose a time to stop everything for 30 minutes. No smartphone, TV, or talking. Meditate on your progress during Days 1-4. Take time to understand your intentions. Dream about your possibilities. Make notes in your journal.

DAY 6

Today have a blessed and no-stress day.

DAY 7

Today just rest.

JANUARY: Week Three

*Wasted time will never be reimbursed,
and it will never propel you forward.*

— Robin A. Hill

YOU WILL NEVER get back wasted time. Pay attention to all the things that you spend time on and assess if that time is being spent wisely. Are the things that you are doing propelling you forward? We all have 24 hours in a day. We sleep six to eight hours a day. Ordinarily, we work eight hours a day. We have eight to ten hours a day to travel, eat, complete daily tasks, be entertained, and socialize.

You should be able to find one or two hours a day to work toward your goals and plans. You can read a book, exercise, eat healthier, listen to an audio book or podcast, write a book, practice something, study, meditate, help someone, create a business plan, get a business loan, study to earn a certificate or degree, organize, mend a relationship, fix yourself up, focus only on being on a heightened emotional level, spend some quality time with the significant people in your life, create, invent, engineer, and so on and so forth. This week only participate in things that support your dreams, goals, and plans.

DAY 1
Today make a list in your journal of a dozen things you will do this week to support your dreams, goals, and plans. Examples of this could be finding more time to exercise, create a budget, have a special family time, take an hour or two and work on something important to you in your business.

DAY 2
Today enrich yourself with information that supports your goals and changes your habits to be productive. Read a book, listen to a podcast, watch a documentary, or take a video course that will support and motivate you toward achieving your plans or goals. Consider making this a regular activity to encourage your personal enrichment and growth.

DAY 3
Today in your journal, write about key points you gained from your enrichment work yesterday. How can you incorporate them in your own plans? Write about that too.

DAY 4
Today consider some new actions you would like to make habits to help you use your time more wisely and benefit from the time spent. List them in your journal. Come back and review them periodically to see how well you are doing in making them part of your life.

DAY 5
Today choose a time to stop everything for 30 minutes. No smartphone, TV, or talking. Meditate on your progress during Days 1-4. Take time to understand your intentions. Dream about your possibilities. Make notes in your journal.

DAY 6
Today have a blessed and no-stress day.

DAY 7
Today just rest.

JANUARY: Week Four

Joy is always positive. Always positive is life being joy.
— **Robin A. Hill**

THERE ARE MANY people and things in life that can potentially discourage you. It is easy to take the route of feeling disappointed and hopeless when things do not go as well as you plan. Taking that easy route is a sign of weakness and immaturity. However, a true indication of strength and maturity is when you are determined to remain positive.

Remaining positive is not always easy, but it's very possible to accomplish. It is the energy that you release that makes a world of difference. Positive energy helps you to remain centered. It creates a smooth, easy flowing environment, and people will respond to you so much better. Energy is power released and will return back in like kind. For example, a smile begets a smile and complaining begets complaints. Positivity houses enthusiasm, optimism, expectation, convinced thinking, and confident speaking. Positivity always attracts opportunities that promote success.

DAY 1
Today say this phrase to yourself throughout the day when a negative thought tries to intrude: *No matter what, I am going to remain positive.* Write this saying in your journal.

DAY 2
Today only think and say what you would like to see manifested in your future. Write your ideas in your journal.

DAY 3

Today focus on how people are responding to you while you are being positive. In your journal, describe what you discover.

DAY 4

Today focus on how you respond to people while being positive. In your journal, describe how this feels to you.

DAY 5

Today choose a time to stop everything for 30 minutes. No smartphone, TV, or talking. Meditate on your progress during Days 1-4. Take time to understand your intentions. Dream about your possibilities. Make notes in your journal.

DAY 6

Today have a blessed and no-stress day.

DAY 7

Today just rest.

JANUARY: Week Five

Stay positive and detach from negativity.

NOBODY'S PERFECT. NO one will interact with you perfectly 100 percent of the time. You will not interact with people perfectly 100 percent of the time. Strive to stay positive when imperfect interactions occur. Remember, everyone wants to be forgiven, including you. The sooner you forgive, the sooner you will mend. In forgiving others, you will be forgiven, and people will favor you. When you do not forgive, you will be negative, and you will not find favor. Negativity houses fear, disconfirming thinking, depression, pessimism, complaining, whining, and turmoil. These create chaos, deprivation, and counterproductive actions.

Negativity causes stress, resulting in you having to work harder to accomplish whatever it is that you intend to accomplish. Negativity weakens determination and bogs down confidence. Even worse, if you are negative, people shun you. The diagnostic lens of negativity only reveals unhelpful patterns, never solutions. *If you do not master being positive, you will never master anything.* This year embrace positivity and be determined to master whatever you put your mind and hands to do.

DAY 1
Today begin practicing a "so what" mindset concerning any negative actions of others. Focus on your own actions and reactions. Make this focus a part of your long-term goals.

DAY 2
Today begin a new habit of saying in your heart "I forgive you" when people mishandle you. Release people of their offenses, even if they do not deserve it. This is for your own well-being.

DAY 3
Today show respect to others, and know that you will reap respect. Respecting others is a direct reflection of your character, not theirs, so make it part of your daily efforts.

DAY 4
Today going forward, at the end of each day, reflect on how well you handled the negative situations that you encountered: the idiotic, senseless, mean, hateful, incompetent, stupid, disrespectful, inconsiderate, selfish, misogynistic, rude, narcissistic, spiteful, or uncaring behavior. List your successes in your journal to remind you of good practices that worked for you.

DAY 5
Today choose a time to stop everything for 30 minutes. No smartphone, TV, or talking. Meditate on your progress during Days 1-4. Take time to understand your intentions. Dream about your possibilities. Make notes in your journal.

DAY 6
Today have a blessed and no-stress day.

DAY 7
Today just rest.

FEBRUARY

Week One

Confidence is expressed when you know what it means. Determination is expressed when you do not stop until you profit from what it means.

Week Two

Always look for truth. There you will find closure.

Week Three

Courage is the springboard that catapults you into the unknown depth of greatness.

Week Four

You are the manager of your mental and emotional state. Not anyone else.

FEBRUARY: Week One

*Confidence is expressed when you know what it means.
Determination is expressed when you do not stop
until you profit from what it means.*
— **Robin A. Hill**

CONFIDENCE AND DETERMINATION are dynamic forces that will rename you and redefine you. Your name will carry the weight of respect and your drive will express your credibility persistently. When you are confident, you never doubt your possibilities. Your determination is the engine that moves with a perpetual force to prove why you are confident. Be confident and determined to do whatever you aspire to do. Make the necessary steps to move forward and do not stop until you succeed. You have heard this said before, "Success is a journey, not a destination." It's true. *The momentum of success is the perpetuation of one goal accomplished after another.* Make one goal after another and have a blissful time watching yourself succeed.

DAY 1
Today in what areas of your life do you feel the most confident? List them in your journal.

DAY 2
Today what do you envision happening in these areas of your life? Describe this in your journal.

DAY 3
Today what good can you do for others in this area of your life? Make a list of two or three things in your journal.

DAY 4

Today share your vision with someone who has a similar vision. In your journal, write about the experience of sharing your vision with someone.

DAY 5

Today choose a time to stop everything for 30 minutes. No smartphone, TV, or talking. Meditate on your progress during Days 1-4. Take time to understand your intentions. Dream about your possibilities. Make notes in your journal.

DAY 6

Today have a blessed and no-stress day.

DAY 7

Today just rest.

FEBRUARY: Week Two

Always look for what is true, there you will find closure.
— Robin A. Hill

IT IS SO much healthier to embrace a matter or to let go of a matter in the realm of truth. There are some things about yourself that you may always need to face. Things that you are not proud to claim. Those things that you really don't want to talk about. Facing the truth about yourself and others is a good place to start and half the battle of getting past obstacles. When facing the truth, you can dismiss lies easily and will not call names or lay blame. There is no hatred, confusion, or entertaining conspiracy theories in the realm of truth. Truth is clear, clean, and settles any matter—whether you like it or not.

DAY 1
Today shine a light on the things that you don't like about yourself, things that you would like to change. These may be weaknesses, bad habits, failures, or obstacles or hindrances that you employ in life that actually sabotage your efforts. Make a list in your journal. Be truthful. Only you see this list.

DAY 2
Today shine a light on the list you made yesterday. Why don't you like those things about yourself? Are you sure they are true? Look to see if you are blaming, hating, or believing lies and conspiracy theories. Write about this in your journal.

DAY 3

Today keep working on the "self list" you created this week. Vigorously look for the truth behind these matters in your life that you listed. Why do they occur? Write about this in your journal.

DAY 4

Today embrace understanding the truths you have examined this week. Now envision yourself changing these weaknesses into strengths. List what steps you would take to make these changes, so you can succeed past your failures, obstacles, hindrances, and problems.

DAY 5

Today choose a time to stop everything for 30 minutes. No smartphone, TV, or talking. Meditate on your progress during Days 1-4. Take time to understand your intentions. Dream about your possibilities. Make notes in your journal.

DAY 6

Today have a blessed and no-stress day.

DAY 7

Today just rest.

FEBRUARY: Week Three

*Courage is the springboard that catapults you
into the unknown depth of greatness.*
— **Robin A. Hill**

IN ORDER TO succeed at anything, you must be willing to change. It takes courage to embrace change, because change hurts. However, you will never succeed doing the same things you have done when you have not succeeded. Accept all that you know, think, and do as a prison of past conditioning. If you want to succeed, be prepared to unload the besetting weight of your past conditioning to experience your irrepressible future of being great at what you do. It's going to take more than the norm to dive into the unknown of becoming great at what you do. Metaphorically speaking, submerging your feet in the water is not enough. It's going to take courage to dive in without hesitation or procrastination.

DAY 1
Today ask yourself what the hardest thing about facing "change" is for you. Write about this in your journal.

DAY 2
Today identify something in your life that is holding you back from an achievement you desire. This can be physically, emotionally, financially, or spiritually. Write about this in your journal.

DAY 3
Today be courageous and make a plan around removing that block to achieve what you desire—and embrace the actions for the change. Write your plan in your journal.

DAY 4

Today in your journal, write how you feel about making your identified change. Write one specific, concrete step you will take immediately toward enacting this change.

DAY 5

Today choose a time to stop everything for 30 minutes. No smartphone, TV, or talking. Meditate on your progress during Days 1-4. Take time to understand your intentions. Dream about your possibilities. Make notes in your journal.

DAY 6

Today have a blessed and no-stress day.

DAY 7

Today just rest.

FEBRUARY: Week Four

*You are the manager of your mental and emotional state.
Not anyone else.*

— Robin A. Hill

AS A CHILD, you are shaped and formed by many people: your parents, teachers, mentors, and guardians. However, when you become an adult, you are then responsible for your own advancement. As an adult, no one is responsible for your behavior but you. You should never stop learning. You should never become an old dog who can never be taught new tricks. You have the power to correct whatever mistakes that were made concerning you as a child. Dwell with all peaceably and show respect, compassion, and mercy. Build your muscles of determination and stay on heightened levels of positive emotions such as encouragement, joy, inspiration, enthusiasm, motivation, and optimism.

DAY 1
Today picture the face that you blame for any bad attitude you might be carrying. Now replace that face with your own face. In your journal, write about what has created this bad attitude.

DAY 2
Today think about the attitude you identified yesterday. Write in your journal about what you need to accept about yourself that contributes to this bad attitude.

DAY 3

Today humble yourself, repent, do whatever it will take to get back to the heightened level of positive emotions. Make a list in your journal of those goals you can implement to improve your overall daily attitude.

DAY 4

Today in your journal, list specific steps to make changes in your way of life to bring more positivity into your life.

DAY 5

Today choose a time to stop everything for 30 minutes. No smartphone, TV, or talking. Meditate on your progress during Days 1-4. Take time to understand your intentions. Dream about your possibilities. Make notes in your journal.

DAY 6

Today have a blessed and no-stress day.

DAY 7

Today just rest.

MARCH

Week One

Every day is a good day, regardless of the rain, pain, and strain of hardship.

Week Two

Your joy is what fuels your strength.

Week Three

Sobriety helps you to win, not lose.

Week Four

Humility is the elevator to use to go up.

MARCH: Week One

Every day is a good day, regardless of the rain, pain, and strain of hardship.

— Robin A. Hill

EVERY DAY IS a good day even if it doesn't go your way. Think about it. We all share the same day. Someone somewhere is experiencing some of the best benefits of life, like getting a promotion, having a beautiful wedding, closing on a new home, making the best love ever, having a baby, or striking it rich. Wonderful things like this are delightful moments and don't happen every day. However, every day the sun is shining on someone and there's always something to appreciate in your day.

Bad mouthing a good day is a true sign of immaturity. Positivity is a true sign of maturity and will empower you to focus on every day being a good day. When things seem to be not as you like, you can exercise patience and hope, because inevitably the things hoped for or other good things are right around the corner. This is why we can consider joy, think big, and reach high during adverse times.

DAY 1

Today mentally prepare yourself to have a good day. Say to yourself, "Every day is a good day even if things do not go my way." Look for large or small positive experiences in your day. List them in your journal.

DAY 2
Today cut through adversity by focusing only on why your day is good. How have you contributed to the good experiences? Describe these contributions in your journal.

DAY 3
Today let your faith be the substance of things hoped for and the evidence of things not seen. Think about how your faith can impact your decisions and choices. List in your journal three ways you especially want to employ your faith in daily living.

DAY 4
Today do not let yourself murmur and complain. Don't jump to conclusions when things don't go your way. Reflect on how you can respond positively in these situations. List two or three ways that you want to practice positive responses more consistently.

DAY 5
Today choose a time to stop everything for 30 minutes. No smartphone, TV, or talking. Meditate on your progress during Days 1-4. Take time to understand your intentions. Dream about your possibilities. Make notes in your journal.

DAY 6
Today have a blessed and no-stress day.

DAY 7
Today just rest.

MARCH: Week Two

Your joy is what fuels your strength.

JOY IS THE key force that will positively enrich any situation in life. Joy is like being in a strong city that cannot be penetrated. Joy is like a shield, an immune system, and an absolute strength that will enable you to be resilient even while experiencing harsh realities. Joy will help you withstand the storms of life. Joy is your insurance policy for keeping your life intact. Joy evicts any dark feeling of emotion. Misery will cloud your mind, but joy enlightens it. Being joyful is choosing to have a fierce attitude in the right direction. Joy is a warm ray of sunshine that dispels the dark, cold, negative realities that we undoubtedly face. Joy is internal from an eternal source.

DAY 1
List in your journal areas in your life where this type of joy exists. Take time to be grateful for each of them!

DAY 2
Today in your journal list areas in your life where this type of joy is absent. Describe what you think are the reasons there is no joy in each of these areas.

DAY 3
Today think about what measures you could take to bring in joy to the parts of your life that need it. List three action items you are willing to take to do this.

DAY 4

Today make the start of your journey to add joy to all parts of your life. Think about the list you made yesterday. What resources will help you make the changes in your daily life? List them in your journal, and then begin to seek them out.

DAY 5

Today choose a time to stop everything for 30 minutes. No smartphone, TV, or talking. Meditate on your progress during Days 1-4. Take time to understand your intentions. Dream about your possibilities. Make notes in your journal.

DAY 6

Today have a blessed and no-stress day.

DAY 7

Today just rest.

MARCH: Week Three

Sobriety helps to win, not lose.

FOR AS LONG as I can remember, there have been people in my life who have used drugs and alcohol to alter their reality. I never looked up to any of them as a winner or role model. Substance abuse can affect a person directly (self-use) or indirectly (use by others). In either case, it is important to find or maintain your own sobriety. Good role models and true winners keep their wits about them. They do not lean on alcohol or drugs. Every person who kicks a substance abuse habit deserves a certificate of accomplishment. They must rebuild their life by keeping their system clean, day after day, year after year.

There is another kind of sobriety: being sober-minded. A sensible person who walks away from a brawl or an argument "wins" that battle. A person who thinks before acting in the heat of the moment wins. Everyone should be the master of their own composure. A person who maintains a clear head and remains temperate never loses and always wins. This winning is powerful and what you want.

DAY 1
Today think back on times when you felt out of control. Was it because you were not sober? Was it because you lost your composure? Write about this in your journal.

DAY 2
Today if you ingest things that alter your reality and sobriety, consider why you do this and write about it in your journal. If being sober-minded is difficult for you, consider why this is and write about it in your journal.

DAY 3

Today think about what you lose socially, emotionally, mentally, financially, physically, and spiritually each time you are not sober. Stop if you have the volition. If lack of sober-mindedness is an issue, think about the cost. Make a list of ways your quality of life is harmed. This might be painful, but be very truthful with yourself. Naming the cost might encourage you to take steps to deal with this lack of control.

DAY 4

Today as you are working through any difficult areas in this arena that might be occurring directly or indirectly in your life, recognize that you may need help. Everyone wants to "win." If you do need help, reach out to someone today. Get the help you need.

DAY 5

Today choose a time to stop everything for 30 minutes. No smartphone, TV, or talking. Meditate on your progress during Days 1-4. Take time to understand your intentions. Dream about your possibilities. Make notes in your journal.

DAY 6

Today have a blessed and no-stress day.

DAY 7

Today just rest.

MARCH: Week Four

Humility is the right elevator to use to go up.

TAPPING INTO YOUR beautiful gifts and talents can, indeed, yield you great success. You can rise to the top. Oftentimes, at that place at the top, it is easy to become arrogant or cocky and a bragger. Humbling yourself will become harder if you are not careful. People are repelled by arrogance and cockiness. We turn a deaf ear to the braggers. What good are your gifts, talents, and accomplishments if you cannot share them with others or no one really cares? That is a very lonely, empty place.

Humility is the right elevator to rise to the top. It will keep you there for many years, and people will celebrate you. You do not have to pat yourself on the back. Others will do that for you. Your gifts, great abilities, and humility will cause the crowd to cheer and people will honor you.

DAY 1
Today take time to reflect on your role in this huge world. This is not to make you feel small. It is to help you see that people are interconnected in so many ways, and that becomes more and more true in this changing world. Share your gifts with honor and joy. Write in your journal about what gifts you can share.

DAY 2
Today think about the many people and things that have contributed to your success. List in your journal at least ten people who have had a major impact on your life.

DAY 3

Today be very grateful for the people on the list you made yesterday as well as any others that come to mind. List the ways these people have helped you and think of ways you can give back.

DAY 4

Today take the time to write a personal note to those who have helped you in a significant way. Thank them and give recognition to the things that have helped you make your own accomplishments.

DAY 5

Today choose a time to stop everything for 30 minutes. No smartphone, TV, or talking. Meditate on your progress during Days 1-4. Take time to understand your intentions. Dream about your possibilities. Make notes in your journal.

DAY 6

Today have a blessed and no-stress day.

DAY 7

Today just rest.

APRIL

Week One

Passion will quench your quest to be great.

Week Two

Success is not a given. It's an option.

Week Three

It's never too late to be great at what you do.

Week Four

The choice is yours.

APRIL: Week One

Passion will quench your quest to be great.

PASSION ADDRESSES YOUR quest, but it will interrupt your life. Your ideas, desire to solve a problem, or make a wrong right will never come to fruition, be solved, or vindicated by living an uninterrupted life. Passion is a drive and an emotion that disrupts the norm for the greater good. Being tired or hungry doesn't matter when you're passionate. You have this unending curiosity for how far you can go to accomplish what you set out to do. Passion helps you think beyond limiting boundaries. Passion doesn't have a quit button or a time clock. Passion couldn't care less about time and agendas. Passion is resilient and has regenerative brakes (brakes that charge your battery). Passion will never be fear, mediocracy, laziness, boredom, self-pity, depression, or bondage. Passion ignites courage, revolution, motivation, revelation, emancipation, inventions, and creations.

DAY 1
Today list in your journal the things you are passionate about, be they large or small.

DAY 2
Examine the list you made yesterday. What are you actively doing that moves any of your passions forward? Write about this in your journal.

DAY 3
Today make a new list in your journal. List the barriers in your life that block your passions.

DAY 4
Today listen to your heart, begin to eliminate the barriers on the list you created yesterday, and begin to move forward purposefully in fulfilling your passions. In your journal, write down what your first step will be.

DAY 5
Today choose a time to stop everything for 30 minutes. No smartphone, TV, or talking. Meditate on your progress during Days 1-4. Take time to understand your intentions. Dream about your possibilities. Make notes in your journal.

DAY 6
Today have a blessed and no-stress day.

DAY 7
Today just rest.

APRIL: Week Two

Success is not a given. It's an option.

I HAVE NEVER met one soul that sincerely wanted to fail. However, I have met many who have and are failing. Sometimes failure is because people involve themselves in things that were not thought out or matched with their purpose for living. Align yourself with things that you are passionate about. Even if you position yourself correctly, success is still not a given without precision, confidence, and determination. To succeed, you have to mentally prepare yourself to deal with the challenges, obstacles, and hindering forces. You have to tell yourself that quitting or failing is not an option. Succeeding is more of a mental challenge than physical. Before you take the first step or action on the physical aspects of succeeding, you must first believe in yourself, envision succeeding, and mentally tell yourself that success is your only option.

DAY 1
Today on a scale of 1-10, how would you rate the success of your career? Your relationships? Write these two numbers in your journal and think about what they mean.

DAY 2
Think about the numbers you wrote in your journal yesterday. Be truthful with yourself and answer the question, "Are you failing or are you succeeding in your career?" How about in your relationships? Write your answers in your journal.

DAY 3

Today if you are succeeding, congratulations to you! Describe in your journal what you attribute this success to. If you are failing—or perhaps think you could do better in one or both areas—no worries, there are always actions that can be taken. Begin by identifying why you believe you are failing. Understanding where the problem lies is a good start. Write about this in your journal.

DAY 4

Today think about steps to take to turn the problems of yesterday's list into positive action. What resources can you connect with that will help you in those failing areas? You might find books, discussion groups, or documentaries or even a mentor or coach that will give you helpful insight.

DAY 5

Today choose a time to stop everything for 30 minutes. No smartphone, TV, or talking. Meditate on your progress during Days 1-4. Take time to understand your intentions. Dream about your possibilities. Make notes in your journal.

DAY 6

Today have a blessed and no-stress day.

DAY 7

Today just rest.

APRIL: Week Three

It's never too late to be great at what you do.
— Robin A. Hill

AS TIME PROGRESSES and we get a little older, sometimes we stop dreaming. We stop dreaming because we stop believing in our capabilities. We stop dreaming because we have gotten lazy and too comfortable. We stop dreaming because we lose the fight in us. We stop dreaming because of fear. Some of us just need our battery jump started. We all have infinite creative abilities that do not die until we die. As long as we have breath, it is never too late to be great at what we do. Take one baby step at a time. Keep moving forward. You can do it. Believe in yourself. Envision doing exactly what you dream about. Your dream may be your divine destiny. There is nothing more fulfilling than fulfilling your destiny.

DAY 1
Today ask yourself which unfulfilled dream you hold is most important to you. Describe it in your journal.

DAY 2
Do you feel you have a divine destiny? If yes, do you recognize what it is? Are you working to fulfill your divine destiny? Write about this in your journal.

DAY 3
Today think about why your most important dream or your divine destiny has not yet been fulfilled. Write about this in your journal.

DAY 4

Today think about what you wrote in your journal yesterday. Be courageous and make a list of baby steps you are willing to take now to begin to fulfill your dream or destiny.

DAY 5

Today choose a time to stop everything for 30 minutes. No smartphone, TV, or talking. Meditate on your progress during Days 1-4. Take time to understand your intentions. Dream about your possibilities. Make notes in your journal.

DAY 6

Today have a blessed and no-stress day.

DAY 7

Today just rest.

APRIL: Week Four

The choice is yours.

DEEPAK CHOPRA SAYS that we are "infinite choice makers" and "bundles of conditioned reflexes." Everything about your life is a result of your choices. We all have the choice to be good or great at what we do. We all have a choice to fail or succeed. We all have a choice to accomplish what we set out to accomplish. We all have a choice to be determined or make excuses. We all have a choice to believe the truth or a lie. We all have a choice to respond or react. We all have a choice to study to give an answer or just give an answer. We all have a choice to be offended or not be offended. We all have a choice to be manipulated or not manipulated. We all have a choice to be happy or not happy. We all have a choice to fulfill our dreams or not fulfill our dreams. The choice is always ours. We have free will, and we live in a free nation.

DAY 1
Today take some time to examine your life. Do you believe you are making good choices in every area? Are there areas where you have difficulty making choices that bring good results? Write about this in your journal.

DAY 2
Why do you think some choices you have made have resulted in unwanted outcomes? Write about this in your journal, being very truthful with yourself.

DAY 3

Today before making a choice, ask yourself if there is one choice that is good for you and those around you. How would this affect some of the choices you have made when the outcome was not as desired? Write about this in your journal.

DAY 4

What steps can you take to make better choices? Write them in your journal.

DAY 5

Today choose a time to stop everything for 30 minutes. No smartphone, TV, or talking. Meditate on your progress during Days 1-4. Take time to understand your intentions. Dream about your possibilities. Make notes in your journal.

DAY 6

Today have a blessed and no-stress day.

DAY 7

Today just rest.

MAY

WEEK ONE

Respect is the reward for great character.

WEEK TWO

Commitment will see you through.

WEEK THREE

Understand your intentions.

WEEK FOUR

Your thoughts form and shape you.

MAY: Week One

Respect is the reward for great character.

SOMEONE ONCE TOLD me that respect is earned not given. We all want to be respected. However, who is standing in line to be disciplined, make sacrifices, or to consider others before themselves? Character is built on the foundation of humility, sacrifice, and discipline. Respect is given based upon our actions. Respect is the cloak worn by those who respond rather than react; by those who adhere to policies and procedures; by those who are empathetic, sympathetic, and compassionate, and by those who respect themselves.

There are those who demand respect, but do not give respect. They are self-centered and feel entitled. Those people are always frustrated, aggravated, and complain about their rights and entitlement. Respect is earned, not forced or demanded. First, you must respect yourself and maintain your dignity. Second, you must have respect for the time, space, money, privacy, business, feelings, and lives of others. Then and only then can you receive your reward of being respected.

DAY 1
In what ways do you demonstrate respect for others? Do you show respect to your spouse and family members? Do you respect yourself? Write your answers to these questions in your journal.

DAY 2
Today identify and list in your journal ways that you can practice offering respect where it is deserved.

DAY 3

Today make a list in your journal of the times that you have been disrespectful. Make a list of the times when you were disrespected. Describe why you think these circumstances happened.

DAY 4

Considering the lists you made yesterday, what steps can you take to become more thoughtful and respectful? What steps can you take to earn the respect of others and allow your character to be developed?

DAY 5

Today choose a time to stop everything for 30 minutes. No smartphone, TV, or talking. Meditate on your progress during Days 1-4. Take time to understand your intentions. Dream about your possibilities. Make notes in your journal.

DAY 6

Today have a blessed and no-stress day.

DAY 7

Today just rest.

MAY: Week Two

Commitment will see you through.

TAKE A LOOK down memory lane. Think about your life where you failed to achieve something you wanted to achieve. I can make a wager that "commitment" was not invited to that party. Think about areas of your life in which you have succeeded. I can guarantee that "commitment" was the DJ laying down the tunes that made the party a success. When you are committed, you are obligated to keep things moving and flowing in the right direction. You are dedicated to an intended cause. If you are unhealthy due to eating the wrong foods, you are not committed to being healthy. If your marriage is failing, one party—or both—is not committed. If you are jumping from one relationship to another, you are not committed. If you are hopping from one job to another, you are not committed to fulfilling your dreams. Dare to dream, and aspire to do great things. Commit to your goal. Commitment will carry you through to the finish line.

DAY 1
Think about the areas in your life where you want to achieve a better result. List them in your journal.

DAY 2
Today review your list from yesterday and write a primary goal you would like to achieve or a specific thing to make better in each area on your list.

DAY 3
Today go deeper on your list for this week. List one to three specific actions you can commit to that will move you closer to creating improvements in your life.

DAY 4

Today is an important day. Take an action from your list yesterday and write about it in your journal. You are taking the first step. When you are ready, take the next step. Commit to moving forward.

DAY 5

Today choose a time to stop everything for 30 minutes. No smartphone, TV, or talking. Meditate on your progress during Days 1-4. Take time to understand your intentions. Dream about your possibilities. Make notes in your journal.

DAY 6

Today have a blessed and no-stress day.

DAY 7

Today just rest.

MAY: Week Three

Understand your intentions.

IT'S ONE THING to have intentions, but it is another thing to clearly understand them. Wisdom is the fundamental truth of a thing. In all of your grasping of knowledge and wisdom, get understanding. You will have a clear path on where to go and what to do. Many times we may have an idea that may spark us, and we are excited about what we intend to do—what our intentions are. Many times the heightened emotions about an idea may be just that—emotions without true intention. Once the thrill is gone, if our intentions diminish too, then what we experienced was not true intention. If your intentions are still in place when the hard work of the idea is upon you, then they are true intentions. Intentions are the life and spirit of a plan. Intentions are the driving force of your purpose.

DAY 1
Today think about why you do what you do. What are your intentions for an outcome? Are your actions pointed in the direction of your intentions? In your journal, write about your intentions for a project or action you are currently working on.

DAY 2
Today look at what you wrote yesterday. As you read it now, do you see clear intentions or do you see emotions about the matter? Write about what you recognize in your intentions. Are they viable? Are you clear about your intent for this project?

DAY 3

Today your goal is to complete or achieve something—to deliver on your intentions—for this project that sparked you. Understanding what those intentions mean will clarify and fortify your desired outcome. Examining your intentions for this project you have identified and finding greater understanding of them can help you be more directed in achieving your goals. In your journal write about one or two realizations that you might have arrived at as you have clarified your intentions on this project.

DAY 4

Today in your journal, consider what you have discovered this week and list your intentions for a different project and action. Do you feel you can be more committed to the new project by exploring clarity in understanding your intentions?

DAY 5

Today choose a time to stop everything for 30 minutes. No smartphone, TV, or talking. Meditate on your progress during Days 1-4. Take time to understand your intentions. Dream about your possibilities. Make notes in your journal.

DAY 6

Today have a blessed and no-stress day.

DAY 7

Today just rest.

MAY: Week Four

Your thoughts form and shape you.

I WAS YOUNG, but now I am much older. For as far back as I can remember, whatever I thought I could do, I did it, believed it, and became it. Whatever I thought that I could not do, I didn't do it. I didn't believe that I could do it, and I never progressed in doing it. Your thoughts are the fertile ground of who you will become. As you waiver, so will your progress. If you want to progress in all that you do, be mindful of your thoughts. Know that you will become the very thing that you think about. If you think that a task or a dream is too hard to accomplish, you are right. If you think that you are great at what you do, you are right. Your thoughts form and shape who you will become.

DAY 1
Today in your journal, list the areas in your life that are not progressing in the manner you wish them to.

DAY 2
Today look at the list you made yesterday. Reflect on each thing you listed, one by one. What are your thoughts and self-beliefs concerning each of those areas? Describe them in your journal.

DAY 3
Today look at your list and the work you did yesterday. Think carefully about each area, one by one. Is there one or more areas on the list that you realize you have no desire to progress in? Take them off your list. Draw a bold line through them. Move on.

DAY 4

Now you have a list of areas in your life where you do, indeed, desire progress. With this amended list, be willing to take fresh steps in your life if you want to progress. Write three specific steps you can commit to take now to make progress in a chosen area. Don't try to do everything at once. This will take time—and commitment!

DAY 5

Today choose a time to stop everything for 30 minutes. No smartphone, TV, or talking. Meditate on your progress during Days 1-4. Take time to understand your intentions. Dream about your possibilities. Make notes in your journal.

DAY 6

Today have a blessed and no-stress day.

DAY 7

Today just rest.

JUNE

WEEK ONE
Effective escapism

WEEK TWO
Direct your time and energy spent

WEEK THREE
Make karma your friend.

WEEK FOUR
Precision is ingenious.

WEEK FIVER
Anger will reveal the hidden.

JUNE: Week One

Effective escapism

YEARS AGO THERE was a famous commercial that said, "Calgon, take me away." It was a hit, and millions of consumers purchased Calgon bath and beauty products to "escape." We enjoy escaping from a stressful day. We love the idea of traveling to get away from the hustle and bustle of life. We all wish to escape our problems. At times, escaping can be therapeutic, but too much of it can be damaging. Some people try escaping in unhealthy ways with alcohol or drugs, This does not work. Our bodies are not designed to ingest poison, too much stress, or bear the burden of too many problems. We need to look for those resources in life to help us think thoughts of peace. We should allow life's circumstances to humble us. Acceptance is the first step in looking for a solution to our frustrations. Being positive will help you escape hustle and bustle in a delightful way. Need help to change? Get help.

DAY 1
Today in your journal, identify areas where you are stressed. How does this stress show up in your life?

DAY 2
Work with the list you created yesterday in your journal. Can you identify specific things—stressors—that cause your stress to build? List the reason(s) why these stressors affect you as they do.

DAY 3
Today think about a typical week. How often are you stressed out? Are there particular stressors that occur more often than others? Write about them in your journal.

DAY 4

Today when stress overtakes you, what do you do to escape? Make a list of your escape mechanisms. Are they constructive? Do they need to be modified? Do you need help dealing with the stress in your life? Write about this in your journal. If you need help, take action to get it. Don't delay. Stress can bring many negative impacts to your life.

DAY 5

Today choose a time to stop everything for 30 minutes. No smartphone, TV, or talking. Meditate on your progress during Days 1-4. Take time to understand your intentions. Dream about your possibilities. Make notes in your journal.

DAY 6

Today have a blessed and no-stress day.

DAY 7

Today just rest.

JUNE: Week Two

Direct your time and energy spent

SOMETIMES I THINK about the wisdom I have now that would have been so very helpful in my twenties and thirties. I know that I would be so much further now if I had that wisdom then. In my forties, I started to feel like my life was being shortened. I started to realize how essential my energy and time spent are to the outcome of my life. If you spend a lot of time and energy on drama, shenanigans, and negativity that will be the outcome of what you will obtain.

If you spend your time focusing on being positive, addressing only the things that are needful for yourself and others, concentrating on the things that will propel you forward, your life will be enriched, and you will be fulfilled. Years ago the United Negro College Fund's slogan was "A mind is a terrible thing to waste." I would like to start another slogan. *Time and energy are terrible things to waste.* Capture every moment like it is your last moment, make it of value and spend it well. Invest in where you will get a sure return.

DAY 1
Today in your journal, create a 24-hour-day chart. Start with 7:00 a.m. and end with 6:00 a.m.

DAY 2
Today think about your normal routine: when you wake up, get your family ready for their day, go to work (even if it is at home), prepare your meals, eat your meals, do chores, run errands, sleep. Add these to the day's calendar you created yesterday.

DAY 3

Today at the end of your day, go to your journal and write in everything else you can think of you have done during the day and evening: chauffeur kids, talk or text on the phone, spend time on social media, watch TV, daydream, work on a home project. Put them in their time slot.

DAY 4

Today review the day's timeline that you created. Have you allowed for proper sleep, time for self-care, quality family time? Are you surprised at how much time you spent doing specific things? Do you need to modify your daily activities to create a better outcome for you? Can you identify areas of wasted time and energy? Write about this in your journal.

DAY 5

Today choose a time to stop everything for 30 minutes. No smartphone, TV, or talking. Meditate on your progress during Days 1-4. Take time to understand your intentions. Dream about your possibilities. Make notes in your journal.

DAY 6

Today have a blessed and no-stress day.

DAY 7

Today just rest.

JUNE: Week Three

Make karma your friend.

WHAT IF EVERYTHING we think, say, and do would boomerang back to us and hit us dead smack in the face? Capturing the idea of a scripture, you will reap what you sow. I think most have heard the phrase, "Karma is a b!^&#." I firmly believe that what you think, say, and do will come back to you in kind. It will most certainly boomerang. I believe it because I see it proven time and time again. For instance, a smile begets a smile, and complaining begets complaints. Haven't you seen a happy person enter a room, and people light up? Haven't you experienced a complainer turning a gathering sour?

I have extended mercy, and mercy has been extended to me. I have given my time and efforts for people, and I find that I am surrounded by people who would do the same for me. I surround my life with truth, and I experience truth. I see people who gravitate to drama and are surrounded by drama. Make karma your friend. She will influence you to be careful about the things that you say, think, and do. She will remind you that whatever you do will come back to you.

DAY 1
Today in your journal, make a list of the things that you say or do that people have told you not to say or do. Why do you say or do them?

DAY 2
Today in your journal, make a list of opinions you have that you know you really shouldn't have. Why do you have these opinions?

DAY 3

Today in your journal, make a list of things you do that you know you shouldn't do. Why do you do these things?

DAY 4

Today study the three lists you have made this week. What damage have these things caused in your life? In someone else's life? Are you ready to make some changes? In your journal, make a list of changes you would be willing to make.

DAY 5

Today choose a time to stop everything for 30 minutes. No smartphone, TV, or talking. Meditate on your progress during Days 1-4. Take time to understand your intentions. Dream about your possibilities. Make notes in your journal.

DAY 6

Today have a blessed and no-stress day.

DAY 7

Today just rest.

JUNE: Week Four

Precision is ingenious.

I GET MOVED emotionally when I think about this subject. It grabs me in my gut. Precision is silent, but so very powerful. It is sexy, breathtaking, and spectacular. It is the distinct difference between extraordinary and ordinary. This is why many athletes and lovers of sport are extraordinary. The ingenious precision of the minds of men and women has gotten mankind on the moon. Has created devices that will blast meteors from hitting the earth. Has gotten aircrafts to fly and race cars to win. It has gotten surgeons to save lives and drones to shoot perfect photography.

Precision makes a world of difference. Use your miraculous mind to be more precise. Do not settle for mediocrity in any area of your life. Precision can help you be socially productive, financially successful, emotionally stable, physically healthy, and spiritually centered. Create that WOW-factor of precision in your personal life. Sharpen your vocabulary and learn to say the right things that will put a smile on people's faces. Precision is work, but it is well worth the effort and well worth the outcome. It is so very exciting and invigorating.

DAY 1
Today in your journal, list areas in your life that are mediocre—neither great nor bad.

DAY 2
Today review yesterday's list in your journal. Would you or others benefit if you improved any areas on this list? Why do you think those areas are mediocre now? Write about this in your journal.

DAY 3

Review the list of mediocre areas in your life and list in your journal any specific, precise actions you are willing to take to enhance one or more mediocre areas. Do something to sharpen yourself. Read a book, listen to an audio book or podcast, practice getting better.

DAY 4

Today in your journal, write about how your life would change if you did enhance one or more of your mediocre areas.

DAY 5

Today choose a time to stop everything for 30 minutes. No smartphone, TV, or talking. Meditate on your progress during Days 1-4. Take time to understand your intentions. Dream about your possibilities. Make notes in your journal.

DAY 6

Today have a blessed and no-stress day.

DAY 7

Today just rest.

JUNE: Week Five

Anger will reveal the hidden.

ANGER WILL SQUEEZE out what is in you and will reveal the hidden. Remember the TV and movie character called the Hulk, the big, green creature that Dr. Bruce Banner turned into? His famous phrase is, "You won't like me when I'm angry." Angry people hurt people physically or emotionally or both. Things said, riding on the wave of anger, can destroy relationships and crush the spirit. When someone is angry, learning and reasoning shut down. In anger, the emotions of love, care, concern, and reason do not function. Mobs are formed and wars are created by angry people. The strength of anger is like a fortress and nothing can penetrate it.

We all feel justified in being angry sometimes, but we must remember that no righteousness is served when we are angry. Righteous indignation cannot be confused with anger. It is not destructive. It is constructive for the greater good. You can allow knowledge to empower you to make the right decision. Never make a decision or have a conversation when angry. Walk away if you can and calm down. Once things are said and done, they cannot be undone. Saying, "I'm sorry" cannot and will not erase the pain, trauma, hurt, and lives lost. History cannot be changed. However, our future path can be changed.

DAY 1

Today in your journal, list what triggers your anger. How often do you get angry in an average week? Write about what happens when you get angry.

DAY 2

Today take time in your journal to write about why you get angry. Write about what you can do to control your anger, to redirect it.

DAY 3

Today think about the most recent time you were angry. In your journal, write about the circumstance, what specifically made you angry, and how that anger showed up. What was the outcome for you? For others?

DAY 4

If you have an anger issue or feel you are developing one, check resources where you can get help. List them in your journal. Carry through and call a professional who might be able to help you.

DAY 5

Today choose a time to stop everything for 30 minutes. No smartphone, TV, or talking. Meditate on your progress during Days 1-4. Take time to understand your intentions. Dream about your possibilities. Make notes in your journal.

DAY 6

Today have a blessed and no-stress day.

DAY 7

Today just rest.

JULY

WEEK ONE

If you are never challenged, are you proven?

WEEK TWO

Learn to compete only with yourself.

WEEK THREE

"Teamwork makes the dream work." (John C. Maxwell)

WEEK FOUR

There are bad apples among us.

JULY: Week One

If you are never challenged, are you proven?

IF YOU ARE never challenged, you cannot claim to be proven. If you are never challenged, you will never build the tenacity to overcome. If you are never challenged, you will never know your true potential. Challenges bring the best out of you and reveal the worst. Challenges can be a motivator or demotivator. Challenges distinguish between the determined and the quitter, the brave and the coward. If not challenged, you will never reach forward. Challenges make the lazy very uncomfortable. Challenges cause you to appreciate the times you are not challenged. Challenges can serve as the stiff kick in the pants that jolts you into action. Welcome your challenges; they will help bring you to your highest potential.

DAY 1
Today make a list of your current challenges in your journal.

DAY 2
Referring to your list of current challenges, describe in your journal what you think is causing each challenge.

DAY 3
Today make a list in your journal of your accomplishments in the past six months. What challenges did you overcome to achieve those accomplishments?

DAY 4

Today think about the challenges you have overcome. Think about the achieved successes. Create a plan to overcome what you identified as your current challenges on Day 1 of this week. You have overcome challenges before, and you can do it again. Write about your plan in your journal.

DAY 5

Today choose a time to stop everything for 30 minutes. No smartphone, TV, or talking. Meditate on your progress during Days 1-4. Take time to understand your intentions. Dream about your possibilities. Make notes in your journal.

DAY 6

Today have a blessed and no-stress day.

DAY 7

Today just rest.

JULY: Week Two

Learn to compete only with yourself.

COMPETITION IS STIMULATING. It gets your adrenaline flowing. The opportunity pumps you to prove what you can do. Don't take your mind off your stride and performance. If you focus on what others are doing, you lose your own momentum and strength. Every second that your focus is on someone else, the energy and keen focus that are necessary to achieve your goals are reduced. You start judging and comparing, which is counterproductive.

Keep your focus on your goal and your potential to go above and beyond your own expectations. Set your mark and, for all intents and purposes, do not take your eye and mind off the finish line. Compete with yourself by telling yourself you can do better, you can go farther, you can achieve what your heart says that you can. The demotivating thoughts will be crowded out and silenced when you encourage yourself. You will plow through the opposition. You will not stop until you accomplish what you set out to do.

DAY 1
Today in your journal, list an area of your life where you are competing for something. What is the importance of achieving the outcome you desire? Describe this.

DAY 2
Today think about the "competition" you wrote about yesterday. Make a list of the significant changes that would occur in your life if you were successful in the competition. Remember, all the changes might not be positive ones. You have to consider those that are not positive too. For example, a promotion might be good

for your career, but that promotion may affect the quality of your family life.

DAY 3
Today you have named the importance of this competition and thought about the changes it might bring to your life. If you "win," develop a game plan to make the most of the positive aspects of winning the competition and reduce any negative impacts.

DAY 4
Today take action on the first step in your competition game plan. Write about whatever you did in your journal.

DAY 5
Today choose a time to stop everything for 30 minutes. No smartphone, TV, or talking. Meditate on your progress during Days 1-4. Take time to understand your intentions. Dream about your possibilities. Make notes in your journal.

DAY 6
Today have a blessed and no-stress day.

DAY 7
Today just rest.

JULY: Week Three

Teamwork makes the dream work.
— John C. Maxwell

IN MY LINE of business, I cannot tell you how many times I've heard the saying, "Teamwork makes the dream work." I have found that it is a true statement. A team is that support group needed to accomplish your goals. Family, coworkers, and friends can serve as a team to help you accomplish your dreams. People who are on your team are imperfect creatures. Trusting imperfect people is not required, but you can trust a proven, functional process. Squash anything that has the potential to divide your team. There will not be one team member who will always handle matters perfectly, including you.

Forgive all who have mishandled you or mishandled a matter. Remember this: *Everyone wants to be forgiven*. The sooner you forgive, the sooner your team will mend and get back on track. *Forgiveness is like a paramedic that gives immediate emergency care to mend the repercussions of human error*. Always keep in the forefront of your mind what you like about your team. Always target solutions to get better as a team. Never focus only on the faults of your team. The momentum, excitement, and thrill of great teamwork ignites a powerful, successful force.

DAY 1
Make a list in your journal of team members who help you in different areas of your life.

DAY 2

Review your list and write down the specific things you appreciate about each of your team members. Take a little extra time to really think about these things you appreciate.

DAY 3

Today consider what you can do to help your team members, show your appreciation to them, or strengthen the team spirit. Write about this in your journal. Even a simple but heartfelt "thank you" is powerful.

DAY 4

Today stay anchored in your appreciation and forgive any team members that need mercy. Take at least one positive action step from your list of what you can do for your team.

DAY 5

Today choose a time to stop everything for 30 minutes. No smartphone, TV, or talking. Meditate on your progress during Days 1-4. Take time to understand your intentions. Dream about your possibilities. Make notes in your journal.

DAY 6

Today have a blessed and no-stress day.

DAY 7

Today just rest.

JULY: Week Four

There are bad apples among us.

WHEN REFLECTING ON the people you have to interact with, you may come across a bad apple or two. Unfortunately, this is prevalent. There are bad apples among us. Bad apples are bad apples for a reason. The weight of your concern is not to get bad apples on track. Tend only to your business unless helping bad apples is your business. I am a compassionate person and have to discipline myself not to take on projects of "fixing" people when they are not my business. Some people may need professional help. These people may be among family, friends, co-workers, management, or leadership. You never have to be subject to wrong doings of bad apples. You can report wrongdoings to the right authorities.

Refrain from acting like a bad apple yourself by reacting poorly to their poor behavior. You can always feel good about doing the right thing, because there are policies, laws, and precepts in place to protect you. What I have experienced is that often bad apples will either separate themselves from you, quit the team, or get fired. Sometimes, you may be moved to a different position. Believe in yourself, stay confident, and be a team player, but do not be swayed by the bad behavior of others.

DAY 1
If there are bad apples in your life, list them in your journal. Why is that person a bad apple?

DAY 2
Today reflect on how you react or respond to bad apples that you must deal with. Describe your actions in your journal. Do you feel your reactions or responses are appropriate for you to maintain a good fair-minded reputation?

DAY 3
Today if you find that you occasionally (or frequently) "react" in ways that escalate in a bad apple situation, what can you do to change your approach to a better on-purpose response? Write about this in your journal.

DAY 4
Today remember this: how you react or respond to a person is a direct reflection of your character, not theirs. Can you think of ways to avoid dealing with the bad apples in your situation or at least minimizing content with them? List whatever ways you can think of.

DAY 5
Today choose a time to stop everything for 30 minutes. No smartphone, TV, or talking. Meditate on your progress during Days 1-4. Take time to understand your intentions. Dream about your possibilities. Make notes in your journal.

DAY 6
Today have a blessed and no-stress day.

DAY 7
Today just rest.

AUGUST

Week One

Judge yourself

Week Two

Proper foundation

Week Three

Meditation: A pathway to succeed

Week Four

Comparison study

Week Five

*"... If you think you can, you will.
If you think you can't, you won't."* (Hendrick Mission Statement)

AUGUST: Week One

Judge yourself

WHEN YOU JUDGE yourself, disputes are resolved quickly, discolored comments are corrected, and you face the truth about yourself. When you judge yourself, you remove the cause for others to judge you. You are considerate. Your social casualties are few and far between. You are accountable for your actions. When you judge yourself, you stay open to the possibility that you could be wrong. You strive to maintain a peace within. You purge yourself from the things that have the potential to disturb your peace. When you judge yourself, you love yourself enough to keep things circulating in your life correctly.

DAY 1
Today know that this week will be one of hard reflection and deep honesty. It's time to take a deeper look into the actions you take. In what you say and do, where do your motives lie? Are they good for you or bad? Good for others or bad? Are your intentions honorable?

DAY 2
Today humbly check the motives of your recent actions. Is there any action that you need to amend? Write this in your journal and when you have made the amendment, cross out the action on your list. This is a process that will take time to accomplish. Review the list periodically, and cross off what you can when you can.

DAY 3

Today think of two to four parameters you can use to help your actions stay healthy, helpful, and considered in any given situation. Replace bad motives with good ones. Make a list of your parameters in your journal.

DAY 4

Consider who you have been to people this week—how you have interacted with them and how they have interacted with you. Keep things circulating in your life correctly. Make notes in your journal of good interactions as well as those that have been less successful. How could you handle the less successful ones better? Write about this in your journal.

DAY 5

Today choose a time to stop everything for 30 minutes. No smartphone, TV, or talking. Meditate on your progress during Days 1-4. Take time to understand your intentions. Dream about your possibilities. Make notes in your journal.

DAY 6

Today have a blessed and no-stress day.

DAY 7

Today just rest.

AUGUST: Week Two

Proper foundation

TO UNDERSTAND THE clarity of your intentions, you must take a deeper look into who you are. Our environment, our experiences, and the people in our lives are among the things that form and shape our foundation. As an adult, you have full authority to make changes if needed. To become accomplished, you will need to strengthen your foundation to withstand the journey. Use your experiences and what you can learn from others to make your foundation stronger. You cannot build a successful life on a faulty foundation, because, eventually, it will collapse. In order to enjoy an accomplished life, it is critical that your foundation be secure. Secure your foundation with knowledge, wisdom, and joy. Never stop learning. Learning helps you to grow and mature. Wisdom comes from learning life lessons and from mistakes made. Choose joy over any dark feeling of emotion. You want to live a life established on the right foundation.

DAY 1
How secure are the foundations of your relationships? Your home life? Your career? Make a list in your journal of what makes your foundations secure.

DAY 2
Today identify any areas of your foundations that might need better securing. In your journal, describe the area or areas that need to be shored up.

DAY 3

Based on what you wrote about yesterday, what steps do you need to take or what resources do you need to build a better foundation? Make a list in your journal and commit to seeking them out.

DAY 4

Today look for the lessons that should be learned from the mistakes of your past. Accept the things you cannot change and discipline yourself to take a more mature approach to building and maintaining your foundation. In your journal, write about the most important lessons you have learned about this.

DAY 5

Today choose a time to stop everything for 30 minutes. No smartphone, TV, or talking. Meditate on your progress during Days 1-4. Take time to understand your intentions. Dream about your possibilities. Make notes in your journal.

DAY 6

Today have a blessed and no-stress day.

DAY 7

Today just rest.

AUGUST: Week Three

Meditation: A pathway to succeed

THERE IS SOMETHING unique about every one of us that people are drawn to. It is up to you to be able to identify your unique abilities and to develop those qualities in order to use them. I have found that meditation can help you discover your inner self. Take time daily for moments of meditation. When meditating, narrow your thoughts to think only thoughts toward gratitude. Release mercy to your offenders, those who have mishandled you, or those who have created negativity in your life. Narrow your intentions to envision only what you want to manifest in your future. Use this time to feel only joy, inspiration, encouragement, and motivation.

Conclude by thinking thoughts of truth. By disciplining yourself to do this process, you will experience a higher level of consciousness, wellness, assertive strength from a silent inner place, a place of peace and solitude, and growth in your creativity. This will help you feel happiness, function with less stress, and, in general, feel more centered. Being more centered is a sure way of being socially productive.

DAY 1
Today take note that you are asked to set aside 30 minutes each Friday with no smartphone, TV, or talking to think and dream. This week, add 10 minutes of meditation with a specific focus each day to see how this feels. After you meditate, feel free to jot notes in your journal.

DAY 2

Today close your eyes and breathe in and out slowly and deeply. Narrow your focus to envision your great future. Narrow your focus to thoughts of gratitude for all the good in your life.

DAY 3

Today close your eyes and breathe in and out slowly and deeply. Narrow your focus to thoughts of mercy by releasing those who have mishandled you or caused negativity in your life.

DAY 4

Today close your eyes and breathe in and out slowly and deeply. Narrow your focus to thoughts of joy.

DAY 5

Today choose a time to stop everything for 30 minutes. No smartphone, TV, or talking. Meditate on your progress during Days 1-4. Take time to understand your intentions. Dream about your possibilities. Make notes in your journal. Add 10 minutes of meditation.

DAY 6

Today have a blessed and no-stress day.

DAY 7

Today just rest.

AUGUST: Week Four

Comparison study

WE ALL HAVE been guilty of performing an unqualified comparison study in our minds about ourselves. As a result of comparing myself with others, I saw myself as being too tall, not tall enough, not having enough fluff in certain places, having too much fluff in other places, not being poor enough, not being rich enough, pretty, not being pretty enough, talented, not being talented enough, smart, not being smart enough. It is human nature to compare. Our capitalistic culture dictates through advertisement how we should look, what we should like, and how we should live.

When we compare ourselves with others, we either make ourselves better or worse than we really are. This is based on how well we have been programmed. We have to be careful not to fall into that mental trap of comparing ourselves or our possessions to that of others. You know the saying, "The grass is always greener on the other side." This way of thinking breeds jealousy and envy. Focus fully on using your gifts, talents, and abilities to their best use. Then you will not have enough time to focus on anything else!

DAY 1
List in your journal the ways you compare yourself to others. Describe how these comparisons make you feel.

DAY 2
Today review your list from yesterday. Did you feel you were "lacking" in any areas on your list of comparisons when you listed how they made you feel? Take time today and describe in your journal why you feel unqualified or lacking in that area.

DAY 3
Today go back to your list of comparisons to yourself. Draw a line through each comparison part. Now look at your list. You will discover that the only thing left standing is the unique YOU!

DAY 4
Today focus only on your unique qualities. Are there any you would like to enhance? Any that you would like to change? If there are, make a list of reasonable action steps to accomplish the enhancement or make the change, and act on them in the coming days!

DAY 5
Today choose a time to stop everything for 30 minutes. No smartphone, TV, or talking. Meditate on your progress during Days 1-4. Take time to understand your intentions. Dream about your possibilities. Make notes in your journal. Add 10 minutes of meditation.

DAY 6
Today have a blessed and no-stress day.

DAY 7
Today just rest.

AUGUST: Week Five

"...If you think you can, you will. If you think you can't you won't."
— **Hendrick Mission Statement**

THINK ABOUT ALL the times that you thought you could do something. Do you remember celebrating your accomplishments? You did not see anything else but being victorious. Think about all of the things that you thought you could not do. How many victory dances have you done concerning those things? I can almost guarantee none. It is a terrible thing to fill your mind with doubt and unbelief. When you are confident, you have no doubt. You believe in yourself. Do not short circuit your success by thinking the wrong thoughts. It is too expensive. Think the right thoughts. You have much to gain. Be determined to profit from what you think about. Your success depends on it.

DAY 1
Today in your journal, identify something that you aspire to do that you have not yet achieved. Describe it. Why do you aspire to it?

DAY 2
Today as you think about your identified aspiration, are you holding any negative thoughts about your ability to achieve this aspiration? If yes, what are they? Write them in your journal.

DAY 3
Today think about your aspiration from only a positive view. Release the doubtful thoughts that you identified and any new ones that come up. In your journal, list specific actions you are willing to take to move toward achieving your aspiration.

DAY 4

In your journal write about what you envision your success will look like and feel like when you achieve this aspiration.

DAY 5

Today choose a time to shut everything for 30 minutes. No smartphone, TV, or talking. Meditate on your progress during Days 1-4. Take time to understand your intentions. Dream about your possibilities. Make notes in your journal. Add 10 minutes of meditation.

DAY 6

Today have a blessed and no-stress day.

DAY 7

Today just rest.

SEPTEMBER

Week One

Our conscience will prick us.

Week Two

Never befriend fear.

Week Three

The love of money or winning rewards "superficialness."

Week Four

People will be attuned.

SEPTEMBER: Week One

Our conscience will prick us.

OUR CONSCIENCE WILL prick us when we handle a matter or someone wrong. The heart is intuitive and has a direct connection with the conscience. It knows the difference between right and wrong. It is not a good thing when you put your conscience away and allow your heart to grow cold. When you are pricked, look for the best solution to make things right. Never sweep a matter under a rug. You will not be able to successfully move forward. People go on, but moving forward and going on are two different things. When you simply "go on," you never resolve a matter, you just go on with unnecessary baggage. When you move forward, you resolve the mishandling, grow past the obstacle, and become a better person. Welcome your conscience to prick you. It's a good thing.

DAY 1
Today reflect on your mishandling of a matter or of someone. What has pricked your conscience lately? Write about them in your journal.

DAY 2
Today think about what made you handle the situation you wrote about yesterday the way you did. How does your conscience tell you to handle it differently? What do you need to do to make things right? Write about this in your journal.

DAY 3
Today think about the things that most often prick your conscience. In your journal, write about steps you are willing to take to alter the behavior or action that causes your conscience problems.

DAY 4

Today make matters right or make things right with people. In your journal, make a list of matters that need to be made right. Revisit this list to check each one off when you have dealt with it. No more unnecessary baggage for you going forward, because now you are willing to alter your behavior or action and grow as a person!

DAY 5

Today choose a time to stop everything for 30 minutes. No smartphone, TV, or talking. Meditate on your progress during Days 1-4. Take time to understand your intentions. Dream about your possibilities. Make notes in your journal. Add 10 minutes of meditation.

DAY 6

Today have a blessed and no-stress day.

DAY 7

Today just rest.

SEPTEMBER: Week Two

Never befriend fear.

FEAR IS COUNTERPRODUCTIVE and a dangerous thing. Never befriend it. It hates you. Fear consumes your heart and mind like a dark, ominous cloud. It will cause you to act in a manner that is irrational, hateful, mean, paranoid, troubled, depressed, or other such destructive behavior. Fear will stop progress. It immobilizes. Fear will stir up hatred, strife, and every evil work. Many people have lost their lives by suicide or murder because of fear. You should never dabble with fear. If allowed to grow, fear eats confidence for lunch and will have determination for dinner. *Fear is the root of prejudice, the path to paranoia, the bread of lunacy. Fear is the bed of a coward, the boa that constricts confidence, the cloak of a quitter.* When you see fear, demolish it before it grows. It is never good to have around. If you see fear coming, go in another direction. If you cannot go in another direction, face it head on without any hesitation or procrastination. It has the potential to grow and kill anything you aspire to do if you don't address it. Don't let fear stop you from moving forward.

DAY 1

Today you will deal with a hard topic in truth. We fear fear and feel "less than" when we experience it, yet it is something that most—even all—of us will experience at one time or another. Think about hesitations, procrastinations, and being stuck. List them in your journal. Is there fear attached to them—fear of being unsuccessful, fear of the unknown, fear of consequences, fear of losing? Maybe even fear of success? Write about this in your journal.

DAY 2
Today look at each area in your list from yesterday and come up with a strategy to tame any fear present. Write this out in your journal. Think about resources and professional services that can support you as you move beyond any fear. This might be a mentor or a coach or it could be learning a new and needed skill. It could be other kinds of professional help. Commit to getting the support you need.

DAY 3
Having a strategy is good, but success requires action. Review the strategy you wrote about yesterday. Turn it into goals and then steps and milestones to meet under the goals. Be specific in ways you can combat fear of action as soon as you recognize it.

DAY 4
Today is implementation day. Take the first step in executing your strategy to take out fear. This is a process to use over and over to see yourself free from fear. Write about your actions in your journal as you take your steps.

DAY 5
Today choose a time to stop everything for 30 minutes. No smartphone, TV, or talking. Meditate on your progress during Days 1-4. Take time to understand your intentions. Dream about your possibilities. Make notes in your journal.

DAY 6
Today have a blessed and no-stress day.

DAY 7
Today just rest.

SEPTEMBER: Week Three

The love of money or winning rewards "superficialness."

HISTORY HAS PROVED that the love of money and only focusing on winning, especially at all costs, puts us in a place that breeds liars, cheaters, manipulators, and combative, contentious individuals. Believe it or not, fear is the reason some people go down this dark path. They are always afraid of losing, and they become very divisive. They lose all sense of honor, respect, and love for themselves and others, because their only motivation is winning or gaining money or both. Don't get me wrong, winning and having money can be very positive. It is the *consuming love* for them that so often causes a negative chain of events. When you find that the love and care and concern for life for yourself and others takes a back seat to gaining money or all out winning, you need to hit the reset button. Maintain your honor, respect, and love for yourself and others.

DAY 1
Today take an honest look at what motivates you. When you strive to do your best or be the best, what is it that motivates you and drives you forward? Write about this in your journal.

DAY 2
Today consider what you wrote yesterday in your journal about motives. Do any of your motives not take into consideration the care, concern, love, or compassion for life, yourself, and your fellow human beings? Are any of them causing you conscience pricks? To act in honor, do you need to change your course or reset your goals? Be honest with yourself and write about this in your journal.

DAY 3

Today take a clear-eyed look at what you have written in your journal the last two days. If you feel you might need a little course correction, what steps are you willing to take to do that? Record them in your journal.

DAY 4

Today ask what is the most significant thing you have recognized about yourself in the past three days? Write about these times in your journal.

DAY 5

Today choose a time to stop everything for 30 minutes. No smartphone, TV, or talking. Meditate on your progress during Days 1-4. Take time to understand your intentions. Dream about your possibilities. Make notes in your journal. Add 10 minutes of meditation.

DAY 6

Today have a blessed and no-stress day.

DAY 7

Today just rest.

SEPTEMBER: Week Four

People will be attuned.

PLEASE DO NOT be misguided by thinking that your unspoken emotional state of being will be inconspicuous. With or without utterance, people will be attuned to your emotional state. Emotions invisibly fill up a room. Usually, we can sense if someone is fearful or confident. If someone is excited, sad, hopeful, glad, not interested, or interested. But we're all guilty of trying to hide our feelings sometimes. We talk a lot these days about individuals (and even companies) being transparent or non-transparent. Some people have developed great skills at being non-transparent as a protection device. Some try to present a "good front" by presenting an emotion they do not feel. Some insincere people alter their emotions to take advantage of someone. They operate under false pretenses, but in most cases, they can do this for only so long before being found out. The truth will eventually be seen. I have found that the solution to all of this is to walk with a clean heart. Strive to keep your emotions positive. Let people feast off of the good fruit of your positive behavior supported by your positive nature.

DAY 1
Describe in your journal how you think your family would describe your general emotional state. How would your friends describe your emotional state? How would your colleagues describe your emotional state? If you can, ask a family member, a friend, and a colleague to tell you how they would describe your emotional state. It may take more than one day to accomplish this. How does what they tell you compare to what you wrote in your journal?

DAY 2
Based on what you have learned from your conversations yesterday about how others perceive your general emotional state, are there any perceived emotions that might need work—emotions perceived other than those that support, encourage, inspire, or motivate yourself or others? Think about what is causing those emotions. What can you do to hit the reset button and get back on course? Write about this in your journal. Revisit these thoughts as you gain more responses. Make an effort tomorrow to hold only positive emotions all day.

DAY 3
Today write about your experience in holding only positive emotions all day. How did this affect your day?

DAY 4
Today create a positive experience for yourself. Take a happy selfie. Take a day trip. Eat a healthy treat. Feel good about your accomplishments!

DAY 5
Today choose a time to stop everything for 30 minutes. No smartphone, TV, or talking. Meditate on your progress during Days 1-4. Take time to understand your intentions. Dream about your possibilities. Make notes in your journal. Add 10 minutes of meditation.

DAY 6
Today have a blessed and no-stress day.

DAY 7
Today just rest.

OCTOBER

WEEK ONE
Never prejudge

WEEK TWO
Seeing things differently

WEEK THREE
Adult tantrums

WEEK FOUR
Connect the dots of life

OCTOBER: Week One

Never prejudge

I AM SURE you have heard the phrase, "Never judge a book by its cover." It is such good advice when applied to people. While a person may present a certain way, you have to wait to see what comes out of their mouth to know who you are dealing with. When people speak, they say what's on their mind and in their heart.

I remember a farmer who went to a car dealership with his daughter. He was wearing suspenders, and his clothes were washed out and worn. All the veteran salesmen avoided him because they prejudged him. A new salesman, hungry to prove himself, thought nothing of it and greeted the man. The farmer represented an organization and told the young rookie that he was there to purchase eight vehicles. That was a great experience for the newbie and a great learning lesson for the veterans.

I met a woman who came to a travel party I was hosting and sat on the corner end of my sofa. She presented as a light complexion African American, short in stature and quiet. When I got to know her, I found out she was a Navajo Indian from New Mexico and her background included being in the US Air Force, an F-16 mechanic, a private duty nurse, an eighteen-wheeler truck driver, and a craftsman. She also had owned multiple businesses, and she was adopted. You will never know who people are until you hear them speak. Get to know the people who come into your life.

DAY 1
Today make a list in your journal of people in your life that you would like to know better. Is the person an acquaintance? Colleague? Perhaps an extended family member? Write down

things you find interesting about each one and things you'd like to know more about for that person. This can prepare you for opportunities for "small talk" when the occasion arises.

DAY 2

Today look at the list you made yesterday and think about opportunities when you can engage with the people on the list. Where and when do you see them? Maybe you can have coffee together occasionally or serve on a committee together or work on a team or project together. When these opportunities arise, ask them about themselves, but don't interrogate them! Be authentic!

DAY 3

As you begin to actively engage with people by really listening to them, write in your journal about those experiences. How did you feel? How did the person feel?

DAY 4

If you are an introvert or are shy, look for another person who might also be an introvert or shy at a gathering where you are, find your courage, and speak to them. You may meet someone very interesting!

DAY 5

Today choose a time to stop everything for 30 minutes. No smartphone, TV, or talking. Meditate on your progress during Days 1-4. Take time to understand your intentions. Dream about your possibilities. Make notes in your journal. Add 10 minutes of meditation.

DAY 6

Today have a blessed and no-stress day.

DAY 7

Today just rest.

OCTOBER: Week Two

Seeing things differently

MOST WOMEN SEE things from a woman's perspective, and most men see things from a male's perspective. Democrats see things from a democratic view, and Republicans see things from a republican view. Church goers see things one way, and non-church goers see things another way. One race of people behaves one way, and another race of people behaves another way. The list goes on and on. This is why we have liberation groups, movements, social wars, big wars, and protests breaking out. Still, despite these differences, as human beings, we have a lot in common. We have the ability to love, have joy, and find peace. We will experience suffering. We can be gentle, meek, and temperate. We have the ability to show respect, care, and concern. Nearly all of us have the ability to show compassion, sympathy, and empathy. We can come together and reason together. We can humble ourselves and know that everyone is not like us, and we can embrace the differences.

DAY 1
Today reflect back to last week. You spent time thinking about listening to people to find out who they are—not judging them by their appearance. Now go a step further. This week be mindful in conversations to listen to the "other side" when someone is presenting a view different than yours. When you interact with someone that is not like you (male, female, race, creed, perspective, or whatever difference), make it a point to listen to and try to understand the situation from their point of view. Write in your journal how this made you feel.

DAY 2

Today reflect on any situation where you find that you have become closed and judgmental. Why has this occurred? Write about these challenges.

DAY 3

Today think about a situation where you and a family member, friend, or colleague hold different opinions. Write in your journal what you think their position is. Be fair! You know what your position is. Can you think of any validity in their different point of view? Are there any points of common ground? Is there a place to "meet in the middle," even if that "middle" is simply to respect the right to hold different thoughts?

DAY 4

Today reflect on what practical steps you can take to bring a workable outcome when you encounter differences of opinion. For example, listen without judgment and seek common ground or a common goal. This is for "little" things as well as for big things! List these in your journal.

DAY 5

Today choose a time to stop everything for 30 minutes. No smartphone, TV, or talking. Meditate on your progress during Days 1-4. Take time to understand your intentions. Dream about your possibilities. Make notes in your journal. Add 10 minutes of meditation.

DAY 6

Today have a blessed and no-stress day.

DAY 7

Today just rest.

OCTOBER: Week Three

Adult tantrums

THINK ABOUT HOW distracting and uncomfortable it is when you see a parent struggling with their child at a store because the child is not getting their way. The screaming, yelling, and falling onto the floor is hard to watch. You can almost hear all the opinions of people who are getting a good earful of the child's rebellious outbursts. When you become an adult, you are supposed to put away childish behavior. You are supposed to be mature enough that if you do not get what you want, you will behave maturely. Unfortunately, many have not matured to this level. Many adults, no matter where they are, have adult tantrums about the things they want and cannot get when they want it. They are harsh, rude, mean, disrespectful, obnoxious, belligerent, aggressive, loud, or otherwise out of control.

We all should welcome circumstances and situations in our lives where we are told "no." At some point in our lives—and likely more than once—we will not get something we want. When this happens, we need to exercise temperance and humility. Our social productiveness depends on it. We have to be able to tell ourselves that it's okay and not the end of the world. Let a "no" motivate you to rethink the situation, try a different solution, or work harder and smarter. Support the person who got the "yes" if it is appropriate and you can. Life is so much more rewarding when we behave that way.

DAY 1

Today think of a recent time that you have lost your cool and had an adult tantrum. Most of us probably have had at least one! Write about this in your journal. Ask yourself if what you wanted was really good for you, good for the circumstance, and good for others. Did you consider that at the time? Can you let it go now?

DAY 2

Today make a list in your journal of circumstances that you think trigger your anger. What can you do to avoid those triggers?

DAY 3

Today write in your journal how you felt after having an "adult tantrum."

DAY 4

Today think about the anger triggers you listed in your journal. If you cannot avoid a trigger, what can you do to change how you respond to it? Write about what behavior or attitude changes you are willing to make to change your response. Thinking about this before an event occurs can prepare you to handle yourself differently.

DAY 5

Today choose a time to stop everything for 30 minutes. No smartphone, TV, or talking. Meditate on your progress during Days 1-4. Take time to understand your intentions. Dream about your possibilities. Make notes in your journal. Add 10 minutes of meditation.

DAY 6

Today have a blessed and no-stress day.

DAY 7

Today, just rest.

OCTOBER: Week Four

Connect the dots of life

DOTS OF LIFE always connect even when it might appear that they don't. Hidden behind the mystery, there is always a reason why dots seemingly appear not to connect. The patterns connect sometimes within lies, deceit, and misunderstandings. We just don't see them right away. If you find that you cannot connect the dots concerning a matter in your life, do not trust what you do not see. Be patient and the mystery will unfold. Remember, truth is transparently glorious, and secrets are secrets for a reason.

Detectives and lawyers spend their entire careers connecting dots. Be your own detective and lawyer. Connect the dots for why you do what you do. Connect the dots for why people in your life do what they do. Connect why you are not successful in some areas and connect why you are in other areas. Connecting the dots is a good way to hold yourself accountable. If you cannot account for why you do what you do, take some time to ponder this. Track your steps, feelings, thoughts, emotions and be true to yourself. There is always a reason why you do what you do.

DAY 1
Today in your journal, list things in your life where the dots just don't seem to connect. Do you know why? What's missing?

DAY 2
Today review your list from yesterday. Is there any area where the dots aren't connecting that simply isn't truly important to you right now? Or that is perhaps not aligned with your primary goals? Perhaps that is an area that no longer needs your attention and you can move on. If so, draw a line through it.

DAY 3

Today review the remaining areas on your list where dots are not connecting. Examine the one most important to you and see if you can create a plan to move forward in that area. Write down your plan and start to implement it.

DAY 4

When you are working on an area where dots are not connecting, you might need to find resources to help you. It is worth the effort to do this. Who or what resources would be helpful to you? List them in your journal and investigate them further.

DAY 5

Today choose a time to stop everything for 30 minutes. No smartphone, TV, or talking. Meditate on your progress during Days 1-4. Take time to understand your intentions. Dream about your possibilities. Make notes in your journal. Add 10 minutes of meditation.

DAY 6

Today have a blessed and no-stress day.

DAY 7

Today just rest.

NOVEMBER

Week One
Spiritual enema

Week Two
Dependency to be or not to be

Week Three
Not my first choice

Week Four
Do your best, then do better

Week Five
Joy and peace of mind

NOVEMBER: Week One

Spiritual enema

WE ALL HAVE to take a spiritual enema from time to time to remove the waste of negativity in our life. There are times in our life when we get impacted with negativity. At times we need a purging. Some people fast and pray. Some people meditate. Both methods have been effective in my life. To purge, you need to focus on being spiritually centered. When you are spiritually centered, you are more focused on health, wellness, and the virtues of life. Sometimes so many trying things happen back-to-back in your life that negative behavior begins to occur. When you feel that happening, hit the reset button. You do not have to be negative. Misery clouds your mind, but joy enlightens it. Being positive filters out negativity.

DAY 1
Today list in your journal the areas in your life that you need to purge and detoxify—actions, activities, people.

DAY 2
Today think about your general attitude. What do you think you are presenting? What do you think other people actually see? Sometimes a good and positive attitude you have worked hard to cultivate can slip or shift in times of trial. List the thoughts that you need to purge and detoxify right now.

DAY 3
Today focus on being spiritually centered. Think thoughts of health, wellness, and the virtues of life. Begin to detoxify and release.

DAY 4

Today if you have been doing your daily reflections, can you feel a difference in yourself as you have been removing and releasing negativity? This is not an instant change, but if you are doing the work, you will begin to feel a difference in your life.

DAY 5

Today choose a time to stop everything for 30 minutes. No smartphone, TV, or talking. Meditate on your progress during Days 1-4. Take time to understand your intentions. Dream about your possibilities. Make notes in your journal. Add 10 minutes of meditation.

DAY 6

Today have a blessed and no-stress day.

DAY 7

Today just rest.

NOVEMBER: Week Two

Dependency to be or not to be

WE COME INTO this world as a dependent. In our early years, we depend on someone for our care, then we must master caring for ourselves and others. Becoming an adult is a progressive occurrence. We learn who and what to depend on and who and what not to depend on. We learn from trial and error. We learn to depend on each other in many ways in society, in relationships, and in work. It is as important for us to be dependable as it is for us to be able to depend on others. Much of this is good and healthy for society and personal connections. However, what we should be wary of is being dependent on people and things to create our happiness.

I have learned it is not wise to depend on things, holidays, or the actions of people to make me happy. It is good to have people in our lives who support, love, and cherish us, but sometimes people will not always support, love, and cherish us. It is not their ultimate purpose to make us happy. People will make decisions that will not favor us, and we will make decisions that will not favor them. We—each of us— must not *depend* on another person to give meaning to our life, even if they contribute to happiness. I have learned to put my trust and dependence on God. People and things will fail us quite often. Don't be dismayed. It's not personal. We all are imperfect people living in an imperfect world. As an adult, here are six things to learn:

- Always be grateful for what you have.
- Always encourage yourself.
- Always humble yourself and look to a greater source.

- Always maintain a forgiving heart.
- Always enjoy your life with or without the support, love, and cherishing of others.
- Always have a Plan B for when people or things are not there for you.

DAY 1
Make a list of all the people and things that you can depend on.

DAY 2
Today think about what you would do without these people and things in your life. Write about this in your journal.

DAY 3
Are you dependable to deliver what you say you will do? Are you sure? Write about this in your journal.

DAY 4
In your journal, write about the ways to take responsibility to create your own happiness and meaning in life.

DAY 5
Today choose a time to stop everything for 30 minutes. No smartphone, TV, or talking. Meditate on your progress during Days 1-4. Take time to understand your intentions. Dream about your possibilities. Make notes in your journal. Add 10 minutes of meditation.

DAY 6
Today have a blessed and no-stress day.

DAY 7
Today just rest.

NOVEMBER: Week Three

Not my first choice

IF A SURVEY was taken, I believe that the majority of the people I know would say they know what they want. However, none of us has a genie in a bottle to make those wants come true. We do not often get exactly what we want. Often we must resort to a second or alternate choice. Here's the important message. We can control being happy about the choices we make. We can do this even if the answer to the "want" is not our first or preferred choice. We can do this by using guidelines around the choices we have to make.

When you need to choose from multiple options or actions, the **4D** Step is a helpful guide:

- **D**ecipher through what is good for you and those around you and select what's best.
- **D**o not compromise your standards.
- **D**o not break any spiritual, mental, emotional, financial, physical, or social laws.
- **D**ecide after ample soul searching, and then accept your decision.

After you have made your choice, move forward. Do not keep thinking back on the subject, but if you need to make a course correction, do it and keep moving. Reflecting on my experiences, I am so happy that I did not always get my first choice. My second choices have often turned out to be wonderful.

DAY 1

Today make a list of the areas in your life for which you have to make a decision.

DAY 2

Today determine whether or not the choice to be made includes the options of alternate choices for each of these upcoming decisions.

DAY 3

Today write in your journal about how you handle situations where your first choice does not happen.

DAY 4

Today write in your journal about a time when an alternative choice that you received turned out to be a wonderful choice.

DAY 5

Today choose a time to stop everything for 30 minutes. No smartphone, TV, or talking. Meditate on your progress during Days 1-4. Take time to understand your intentions. Dream about your possibilities. Make notes in your journal. Add 10 minutes of meditation.

DAY 6

Today have a blessed and no-stress day.

DAY 7

Today just rest.

NOVEMBER: Week Four

Do your best, then do better

DR. MAYA ANGELOU said, "Do the best you can until you know better. Then when you know better, do better." The ceiling that is over our heads is sometimes a ceiling that we put there ourselves. Never stop with knowing that you did your best. Always tell yourself to learn more. Always tell yourself to do even better. My husband said to me once, "Time is life and life is time." Tell yourself that time is of essence, so don't waste it. Remove arbitrary ceilings from over your head.

Let the sky be the limit to what you can do. If you begin this mindset when you are young, you set yourself up for life. When you get older, the comforts and conveniences of life will be waiting for you. If you have not yet created this mindset, start now! When is the best time to accomplish something? Right after you've just accomplished something. You are motivated, pumped, enthused, inspired, and want to taste victory again. It is motivating.

DAY 1
List in your journal the areas in your life in which you feel you are doing your best. Take time to appreciate and enjoy your achievements, the things you are pleased with having done. Recognize them for what they are!

DAY 2
Today as the good feelings linger from creating your achievements list, think about how you were able to do these things. Make a list of actions and attitudes that contributed to your successes.

Explore them a bit. How could you use them to create other successes in your life?

DAY 3

We've all heard of glass ceilings and, likely, we have created a few ceilings over our own head. Is there something in your life at this time that would benefit from breaking any ceiling you have imposed on yourself? Explore the liberties of not having a ceiling over your head. Reach high and think big. Write about this in your journal.

DAY 4

As you have been working through the reflections in this book and journaling along the way, can you see ways that your mind and heart have expanded? Can you see ways that rethought behaviors and responses have improved your quality of life? These are successes at breaking ceilings. Write about these changes and be filled with joy for what you have accomplished!

DAY 5

Today choose a time to stop everything for 30 minutes. No smartphone, TV, or talking. Meditate on your progress during Days 1-4. Take time to understand your intentions. Dream about your possibilities. Make notes in your journal. Add 10 minutes of meditation.

DAY 6

Today have a blessed and no-stress day.

DAY 7

Today just rest.

NOVEMBER: Week Five

Joy and peace of mind

LIFE INEVITABLY WILL include trouble, turmoil, tribulations, devastation, and setbacks somewhere along the way. Probably most of us expect it. The question is, how do we combat these challenges when they arise? How do we free our minds from fault and blame for ourselves and for others? Where do we get the strength to pick up the pieces and move forward? Inner peace and joy will help you overcome. Think of the things that are lovely, honest, and just. Think about the virtues of life. Think of the people and things that are praiseworthy. Think thoughts of gratitude. Think thoughts of hope. You will find that peace of mind will keep your heart full. You will find that joy and laughter will scatter the clouds of darkness.

DAY 1
Ask yourself if there are people in your life that you blame for some circumstance you have experienced or are experiencing. Has something happened or not happened in your life or the life of someone else that you blame yourself for? List the people and the circumstances in your journal.

DAY 2
Today take time to think about each of the circumstances and people on your list from yesterday, one by one, and release the feelings of blame that darken your mind and heart. Release your own blame too. This may take some time to accomplish releasing them one by one. Try to remove everything from your blame list over time. If something new comes on it, release it and let it go. Blame solves nothing.

DAY 3

Today as part of releasing blame, what can you do to move forward? When you start to lay blame, be it on yourself or someone else, what steps can you take to move toward positive action? Write about this in your journal.

DAY 4

Today think only of the right things. Think of things that are lovely, honest, just, virtuous, and praiseworthy. Who exemplifies these virtues in your life? Make a list of these people and when tribulations come, large or small, think of their positive influence in your life and in the world. Let these thoughts fill you with peace and joy. Let them edge out blame, anger, disappointment, and other unhelpful feelings.

DAY 5

Today choose a time to stop everything for 30 minutes. No smartphone, TV, or talking. Meditate on your progress during Days 1-4. Take time to understand your intentions. Dream about your possibilities. Make notes in your journal. Add 10 minutes of meditation.

DAY 6

Today have a blessed and no-stress day.

DAY 7

Today just rest.

DECEMBER

WEEKS ONE TO FOUR

*And in the end, it's not the years in your life that count.
It's the life in your years.*

— Abraham Lincoln

DECEMBER: Weeks One to Four

And in the end, it's not the years in your life that count. It's the life in your years.

— Abraham Lincoln

THE THINGS THAT matter in our lives are the things that should count the most and receive the most focus. They are the things that make a difference. They are the things that enrich us. They are the things that help us accomplish our dreams. They are the things that catapult us into fulfilling our divine purpose. They are the things that help us build a legacy. They are the things that remind this world of why we exist.

Measure your life by what counts. I hope *52 Weeks of Purposeful Thinking* has helped you make a good start in clarifying your life and purpose. You are stronger now, understand yourself better now, and have begun to free yourself and others from burden and blame. You have taken the time to think about joy and happiness, to gain peace of mind, and to build a positive attitude. You have done so much work to accomplish this!

In the busyness of this season, set aside at least 30 minutes every single day this month to pause, be still, and appreciate all the good in your life. Let your heart be filled to the brim with gratitude and praise. Meditate on the goodness of God and allow His goodness to permeate your entire being.

Every day . . .

- Be grateful.
- Appreciate your loved ones and your friends.
- Mend anything that needs mending.
- Give something to the people you value in your life—a smile, encouraging words, your time, a card, gift, a flower, etc.
- Forgive and show mercy.
- Slow things down, pray and meditate.
- Review your whole journal and celebrate yourself for all that you have explored and accomplished this year.

Your good work has started, but you are never finished with change! There will always be work to do! There may well be good habits you desire that you have not yet accomplished. They will be working for you in the coming year. For now celebrate, be thankful, and stir your joy. Always be ready to move forward. Hold all the warmth and good cheer of this season as you go into the new year ready to conquer the negative, accomplish the positive, and fulfill more dreams. Merry Christmas and Happy New Year!

About the Author

Co-Founder of Wellness Today Inside Out, Robin A. Hill for decades has been involved in the care and development of others. She attended TEIA School of Ministry and received her degree in Biblical Studies. She became licensed and ordained in 1993 and has been on the move ever since. As School Administrator, she raised up a Christian Academy from k-4 through 12th grade. She served as the school's Senior Advisor for 14 years.

In 2007, Robin relocated to North Carolina and started a new chapter in her life. She began her work in the auto industry, where she has created a great network with her community. In 2019, she was honored by CDK Global and "Auto Remarketing" magazine for her excellent service. "Auto Remarketing" and "AutoSuccess" magazines highlighted her successes again as an author and a Joy Specialist.

In February of 2021, Robin launched Women Empowerment sessions through Wellness Today Inside Out. Currently women from across the nation are joining in. In 2021, Wellness Today Inside Out held a very successful inaugural Single Women's Retreat. In 2022, Robin founded the Lady Lexus Club in Charlotte, North Carolina. She is also a sought after Motivational Coach.

Robin is author of multiple books. She released her first book *Urban Joy in 2013*. She published her second book *The Making of a Beast in 2021*. In 2022 Robin created a book/workbook *Grown Folks Business/ Marriage Can Work* exclusively for the Marriage Retreats/Couples Sessions that she and her husband hold. Her fourth book, *52 Weeks of Purposeful Thinking*, was created for the many who have expressed a need to stay on course to fulfilling their dreams and aspirations. Robin is working on her fifth book. *Urban Joy Ever After* is being written to help people live a joyful quality life until eternity..

Robin is married to a supportive, loving man, R. Alonzo Hill (Founder of Zolingo's Spice For Life). Robin serves as a consultant of his company and as Travel Agent for Spice For Life World Travel. Robin has two beautiful daughters, two great sons-in-law and five beautiful grand babies. Robin's favorite pastime is enjoying nature and loving her beautiful family.

To learn more about Robin and her work, visit any of the following:

- wellnesstodayinsideout.com
- makingofabeast.com
- zolingosspiceforlife.com
- spiceforlifeworldtravel.com.

For bookings please call 980-202-0807.

www.ingramcontent.com/pod-product-compliance
Lightning Source LLC
Chambersburg PA
CBHW050727010526
44107CB00009B/768